The
New
Disciple

Arline J. Ban
and
Joseph D. Ban

The
New
Disciple

JUDSON PRESS
Valley Forge

THE NEW DISCIPLE

Unless otherwise indicated, Bible quotations in this volume are in accordance with the Revised Standard Version of the Bible, copyrighted 1952 and 1971 by the Division of Christian Education of the National Council of the Churches of Christ in the United States of America, and are used by permission.

Other versions of the Bible quoted in this book are:

The New English Bible (NEB), Copyright © The Delegates of the Oxford University Press and The Syndics of the Cambridge University Press, 1961, 1970.

Good News for Modern Man (TEV), Today's English Version of the New Testament. Copyright © American Bible Society, 1966, 1971.

Library of Congress Cataloging in Publication Data

Ban, Arline J.
    The new disciple.

    SUMMARY: A discussion of what it means to be a disciple of Christ in today's world aimed at young people who are thinking about joining an American Baptist church.
____ _____ Leader's guide.
    Bibliography: pp. 47-48.
    ISBN 0-8170-0706-7

    1. Baptists—Membership—Juvenile literature.
2. Christian life—Baptist authors—Juvenile literature.
3. Baptists—Doctrinal and controversial works—Juvenile literature. [1. Baptists—Membership. 2. Christian life—Baptist authors] I. Ban, Joseph D., joint author. II. Title.
BX6219.B35   248'.48'61   75-35898
ISBN 0-8170-0658-3

To our children: Susan, David, and Deborah Anne as they search for new understandings in Christian discipleship.

Contents

A Few Starting Words

The New Disciple is written for young people who are thinking about joining an American Baptist church. If you are interested in finding out what it means to be a disciple of Christ in today's world, the following pages may help you.

The material begins with the first step of discipleship 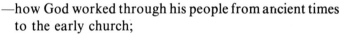 the commitment to God in Christ.

The following chapters consider:

—how God worked through his people from ancient times to the early church;

—how the early church grew through the years to become the many churches known today in America and around the world;

—what is important in understanding your church;

—what it means to be a Christian.

The New Disciple is a study workbook that you can use by yourself or with other young people. It will not always give information. There are places where it asks you to answer questions, and you will have time to record how you think and how you feel. There are times you will investigate and report information—for only you can gather certain facts.

Sometimes you will need to "talk over" the questions with others. Discuss them with your pastor, parents, or other church friends. Then make up your own mind as to what the answers may be for you.

Bible study is a part of this workbook. You will be involved in searching the Scriptures to find information. Also, there are stories or case studies of people who have given witness to their faith.

Each chapter has the section "Some Things for You to Do." In it are suggestions for activities. They may be fun for you to do and, at the same time, may help you learn about the Christian faith. You may want to do some activities alone, or you may choose to include others.

This study really begins with you. Where are you in your faith? Before you begin, fill in the section entitled "Before You Begin Your Study." Then, continue to discover what it means to be a new disciple.

Gospelels Mattew Mark Luke Jhon (handwritten)

Before
You
Begin
Your Study

Mark the number which describes what *you* think about the questions listed below. A "5" would mean it's very important. A "4" would mean it's less important and so on down to a "1" which would mean it's not very important.

1. How important is the Bible to the Christian faith?

    (5)   4   3   2   1

2. How important is belonging to the church to being a disciple of Christ?

    (5)   (4)   3   2   1

3. How important a difference does being a Christian make in the world in which you live?

    (5)   4   3   2   1

List three things which you consider to be the business of the church. to learn (handwritten) To kNow about God (handwritten)

Write several words to describe how you feel about the church.

Write questions you have about being a Baptist.

In a few words, tell your reasons for joining this class.

11

1

Discovering the Meaning of Commitment

"Look Out, World—Here I Come!"

Growing up in today's world is an exciting adventure! There are many choices you will need to make:

what kind of person you will be;

what kind of friends you will have;

how you will use your time;

how you will develop your special abilities;

how you will use your "specialness."

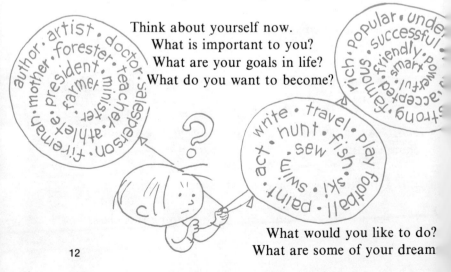

Think about yourself now.
What is important to you?
What are your goals in life?
What do you want to become?

What would you like to do?
What are some of your dream

There are many influences that help to shape
  what you will become
        and
  what dreams will come true for you.
     Your friends,
    your school experiences,
  the neighborhood in which you live,
    the groups to which you belong . . . all influence you.
What are some of the clubs and groups you belong
to now? Check them below:

        Scouts

        4-H

        Campfire Girls

        Rainbow

        "Rock" group

        Drama club

        Others? List them.

As you continue to grow, there will be many groups that ask for your loyalty. You will have many choices to make. The most important choice you will have to make is whether or not to belong to the
        CHRISTIAN COMMUNITY!
Joining this community is different—special—like no other membership!

> **Requirements for Membership in the Christian Community:**

    Lifelong commitment
        • to Christian discipleship and
        • to the people of God.

This is a big order and often takes years to understand fully. Let's begin by defining the word "commitment."

Word Study: Commitment

How would you explain commitment in your own words?

When you are asked
   to be committed to a task
      or
   to be committed to a group,

what does it mean?

> **com-mit-ment:**
> **taking upon oneself**
> **a personal responsibil-**
> **ity toward other per-**
> **sons.**

The following stories are about people who understood commitment. Read each story. Then think about ways commitment showed itself in each situation.

– 1 –

Jim was a good basketball player. But studying for him was difficult. Jim knew he had to have a good grade average in order to stay on the high school team. Basketball practice was every afternoon after school. The games were held either in the evenings, on Saturdays, or after school. That kind of schedule left little time for Jim to do his schoolwork. He made the decision to try to be both a good player and a good student. This meant he disciplined himself to go to bed earlier than usual every night so that he could get up early in the morning to study his schoolwork.

- How does commitment come into play in this story?
- To what was Jim committed?

"An athlete who runs in a race cannot win the prize unless he obeys the rules" (2 Timothy 2:5, TEV).

– 2 –

A Woman in History

Joanna P. Moore lived over a hundred years ago. She was an unusual woman with a daring spirit that led her to do work never done before. Joanna P. Moore was aware of the problem of blacks before other men and women of her time were. Before the Civil War ended, she went to work with the black women and children on Island Ten in the Mississippi River. She had no salary. Her home church, the First Baptist Church of Belvidere, Illinois, sent her four dollars a month to cover her expenses. The government promised her transportation and a few rations.

Joanna P. Moore thought of a simple way to help persons read, write, and learn about the Christian faith. Her plan was for mothers and children to teach each other the basic facts of reading and writing. They usually sat around the fire. In its warmth and light they read to each other. "Fireside schools"— as Miss Moore called them—sprang up all over the South.

Other people did not encourage her work. Many times she could not find transportation because she was going to a meeting of blacks. In Baton Rouge, Louisiana, she was forced to close a school, pressured by people who didn't approve of her work with blacks. She wrote the following letter in the late 1800s:

We hear much about the Negro problem. God has given his children a guide book which makes the path of duty very plain. The white man blames his black brother because he wants to be free. Yes, free like other men, free to vote, to hold office, enter public houses, stay in any hotel, eat at any lunch house, ride on any street car, sit in waiting rooms, worship in any church, in short, be as free as any white man in the same position. The black man could not see how the simple color of his skin should make any more difference than the height or weight, color of hair or eyes of white people made as respects their treatment of each other. The guide book teaches us to quit talking about race, master of slaves, and to bury the whole past and strive to help each other to be God's free man. There is no problem before me, I know what to do. First, be good, loving, helpful and cheerful myself. Comfort others. Divide my last slice of bread with the hungry, cheer the fainthearted, tell them God lives and God loves.[1]

In 1877, Joanna P. Moore was the first woman commissioned by the Woman's Baptist Home Mission Society.

- What are some things in the story that tell about Joanna P. Moore's commitment?
- What were the reasons she did what she did?

". . . like the Son of Man, who did not come to be served, but to serve and to give his life to redeem many people" (Matthew 20:27-28, TEV).

– 3 –

A Man of Faith

In Old Testament times, Abraham, as a young man, lived in a city called Haran. As was the custom in those days, Abraham and his wife lived with his father and the other members of their tribe. Abraham probably had an easy life living there. For an ancient city, Haran was well developed. It had many advantages over the surrounding desert lands. The people of the area had many gods. They worshiped the stars. They made gods of the planets, the sun, and the moon. Many temples in the city were dedicated to the moon god. Abraham did not believe in honoring these many gods. He worshiped only the one true God. God spoke to Abraham. God promised that if he would leave Haran and move to another country, Abraham would become the father of a great nation. Abraham had everything to lose—an easy life, the comfort of his father's home, and the security of the city. But he left with his immediate family to wander as a nomad. Abraham had faith in God and God indeed led him. From his family came the Hebrew nation.

[1]Faith Coxe Bailey, *Two Directions* (Rochester, New York: Baptist Missionary Training School, 1964), p. 25.

- What did Abraham's commitment to God demand of him?

". . . faith did not leave him, and he did not doubt God's promise; his faith filled him with power, and he gave praise to God" (Romans 4:20, TEV).

Compare the three stories you've just read.
- How are they alike? How are they different?
- How are the following ideas found in the above stories of commitment?

discipline
  faith
    goals
      freedom
        action
          sacrifice
            decision making
            loyalty

- In the list above, check those words you need to know more about.
- Think of people you know who are committed to a group or an idea. What other words can you add to the above list that describe commitment?

The Commitment of Jesus

Joining the Christian community requires a commitment to Christian discipleship. Christian discipleship is another big idea. We might say that it means

being a decider for Jesus,
or
being a follower of Jesus,
or
accepting Jesus Christ as
one's Lord and Savior.

These phrases really mean that in Christian discipleship we follow Jesus Christ in our commitment to God.

Jesus was committed to do the will of God. By means of a Bible study, let's discover what commitment meant to Jesus. *Read* Luke 2:39-52. Jesus—a decider!

Mary and Joseph followed the law of the Old Testament. They dedicated Jesus to God when he was a baby. At the age of twelve, Jesus made his own decision about the direction of his life.

• What decision did Jesus make?

Read Matthew 3:13-17. This describes Jesus' baptism.

• Why did John object to baptizing Jesus?
• What reason did Jesus give for being baptized?

Read Matthew 4:1-11. This tells about the temptations of Jesus.

Following his baptism, Jesus went away by himself to think about his mission. He needed to think through how he would live out his commitment. Jesus knew he

> **Mes-si-ah:**
> **the expected king and deliverer of the Jews.**

was the Messiah. He was aware of the divine power God had given him. Jesus had to plan how he would use his life and power to do God's will. The temptations picture the kinds of choices he had to make. The answer he gave to each temptation comes from the Book of Deuteronomy in the Old Testament. Jesus knew the Old Testament Scriptures well enough to quote them. He talked about what had happened to the Hebrew people in Old Testament times.

• What was the first choice Jesus had to make? (v. 3).
• How did he choose?
• What was the choice put before him by the second temptation of the devil? (vv. 5-6).
• If Jesus lived in our world today, how would he be tempted to tell the world that he had supernatural powers?

- How did Jesus decide?
- In the third choice (vv. 8-9), Jesus was tempted to give in to evil and do wrong as a way of gaining power in governments and lands and over people. How would you describe his answer?

Read Luke 4:16-19. This tells about Jesus' teaching in Nazareth.

Jesus began his ministry in Nazareth. His first sermon explained what his ministry was going to be. Jesus had a revolutionary message for the people of his time. It upset people then and continues to disturb people now!

- Who are some of the people Jesus is concerned about?
- What kind of problems was he facing?
- What changes do you think he wanted to make?

Read Mark 2:15-17. This tells more about Jesus' ministry.

The "religious people" of Jesus' time did not understand his ministry—Jesus was sharing a meal with publicans and sinners. The sinners were people who failed to keep the Law as it was outlined in the Scriptures. They also ignored the set of rules about clean and unclean foods. These rules were set up by the religious order of the Pharisees. The publicans collected taxes for the ruler, Herod Antipas. They were hated by many people. The publicans were believed to be dishonest men. The Pharisees thought the publicans and the sinners were unrighteous. They would not be seen with them. The Pharisees would not associate with them in *any* way. Jesus "shook up" the Pharisees. Jesus claimed to be a religious teacher. They thought: "How could Jesus allow himself to be in the same company with those kinds of people? They are publicans and sinners!"

In these verses Jesus lends understanding to his calling.

- What does he mean in these verses?
- How does he answer the Pharisees concerning his mission?

> **mis-sion:**
> **something a person takes upon oneself to accomplish.**

- What do these verses say about the mission of Christians today?

Jesus had some new ideas. He was an attractive young leader. His message was different and practical. The kingdom of God he talked about had more to do with feeling and caring for people than with worrying about following all the religious rules. There were probably many people who heard him who wanted to join up with his group right away and be a follower.

What Jesus required was not easy. To be a follower demanded complete commitment to his mission.

Read Luke 9:57-62. Jesus tells what he requires.

- What does Jesus require of his followers?
- Does Jesus mean that a follower will not have a home?
- Does he mean a disciple must forget about caring for one's family? Why or why not?
- What is the meaning of commitment that Jesus is trying to make clear?

Be a Jesus Decider!

The call to commit oneself to God in Jesus Christ is as real today as it was in the first century. The presence of God is always inviting us to accept Jesus Christ as Lord and Savior. God speaks today in many ways.

How do we hear the invitation?

Through people,

through experiences,

through everyday happenings!

Sometimes the invitation comes in a special way

—with a Christian experience that is exciting and real.

Sometimes it comes through the influence

—of a Christian family.

Sometimes it comes through persons

—especially people who live in a Christian way.

Sometimes it comes through a conversion experience

—a changing over
from
one style of living
to a
different style
of
Christian living.
However the invitation comes,
it is a choice to
accept Jesus Christ as Lord and Savior and

join the Christian community!

To be in Christ means
—commitment to the people of God and
—to be a member of the Christian community.
Commitment and community are both part of one decision.
By accepting Jesus Christ, you become a part of a living

Christian community, the church of Jesus Christ.

This commitment begins a lifelong process, a kind of
growing that takes a lifetime. It means
BECOMING   a mature person . . . through searching
and learning;
RELATING   to others in personal ways . . .
feeling,
accepting,
caring,
sharing,
loving,
giving,
receiving;
CELEBRATING   life together . . .
learning,   sharing the communion meal,
singing,   welcoming new members,
praying,   baptizing,
playing,   laughing;

SERVING   others . . . in
    the home,
        school,
            the neighborhood,
                the country,
                    the world.

In the following pages of this workbook you will discover more about becoming a Christian.

Some Things for You to Do:

1. Research one of the following Gospels: Matthew, Mark, or Luke. Look for:
   What did Jesus want in a follower?
   What does one have to do to be a disciple? (One clue: Luke 9:57-62.)
   To be a disciple means:

2. Interview people in your church: Choose people of different ages. Find out what Christian commitment means to them. Think ahead about the questions you will ask. Record their ideas. Use a tape recorder or write down what they say in the space below.

3. Hold a Family Round Table Discussion: have a "talk session" with the members of your family. Discuss: What does it mean to be a Christian? Record the ideas of each member. NOTE: A very young child in the family might understand this question as "How can we be like Jesus?"

2
Where
It All
Began

When you join the Christian church, you will belong to a people with a long history. This chapter explores God's commitment to his people from the early times of the Old Testament to New Testament Christian beginnings.

Some Things to Think About:

Where did we get the idea for a church?
Where did it begin?
Who started it?
What special things happened along the way?

A Place to Begin: the Bible

The Bible tells us of the beginnings of Christianity. Let's examine it.

The Bible is a collection of books. Ever count them all? Look at the table of contents in your Bible.

How many books are there?

What are the two big parts of the Bible called?

The Old Testament books tell about God and the people who worshiped him before the time of Jesus. The New Testament books tell about God and Jesus and the people who lived after Jesus. The *key* idea in both the Old and New Testaments is how God kept his *promise* to the people who followed him.

The many books of the Bible were written over hundreds of years. They were written about a different time in history than the world we live in today. Sometimes the words or ideas that are used may seem strange to us who live in the modern world. There are reference books, however, to help us to use and understand the Bible.

You may look up the following reference books in your church library or in the public library. Find out how they help you understand the Bible.

	Write the title of one below:	How does it help?
Bible atlas:	_____	_____
Bible dictionary:	_____	_____
Bible concordance:	_____	_____
Bible commentary:	_____	_____

The Bible tells the history of a people who, in a special way, followed the leading of their God. The Old Testament history begins with a story of a man named Abraham, a chief of a tribe. God worked out a special relationship with Abraham. God called Abraham to leave his home country and go to a new, unknown land. The special way God and Abraham carried out their business together was called a *covenant* relationship.

A covenant is
  a promise one person makes
  to another person, and that
  promise is kept for as long as
  both live.

> cov-e-nant:
> a formal, solemn, and binding agreement, treaty, or pact.

The closest thing to a covenant we see in everyday life is
  two people happily married for many years,
                    or . . .
  a treaty of long standing, such as the peace treaty between

the United States and Canada; it has been faithfully kept without the need for armies.

What other examples of a covenant relationship can you think of?

A Self-Study of the Bible

You can follow Abraham and his descendants through the books of the Bible. Abraham was called the father of his people.

Read Genesis 12:1-3.

- What is Abram asked to do?

- What is he promised?

- Who makes the promise?

For the change of the name of Abram to Abraham, see Genesis 17:1-8.

Isaac was the son of Abraham. Jacob was the grandson.

Read Genesis 32:28.
- What name was given Jacob?

Read Genesis 35:23-26.
- Who were the twelve sons of Jacob?

> **Is-ra-el:**
> the name Israel means God strives or God rules.

Jacob's sons were the founders of the twelve tribes. These twelve tribes of Israel in time settled in the Promised Land. Long before that, however, a famine forced Jacob to lead his clan into Egypt; they remained there for a long time. After many years, a new ruler, or Pharaoh, came into power. The Egyptians made slaves of the Hebrews and put them to hard work.

Read Exodus 1:8-14 and 3:1-12.

This describes Hebrew slavery. Even in their hard times, God looked after their needs. Hearing their cries, the Lord urged Moses to go back to Egypt. Moses was sent to lead the Hebrews out of captivity and into freedom.

- How did God speak to Moses? What attracted Moses' attention?

- What did God want Moses to do?

- Who was Moses to say had sent him to the people of Israel?

The flight of the Hebrews out of Egypt toward freedom was called the *Exodus*.

> **ex-o-dus:**
> **the word literally**
> **means "road out."**

The Covenant Promise

Later, at Mount Sinai, God gave the Ten Commandments to the Hebrew tribes. In this way, God kept his covenant promise to Abraham.

Read Exodus 20:1-17.

- What are the Ten Commandments? Rewrite them in your own words.

For many, many years, before they could enter into the land God had promised to Abraham, the twelve tribes wandered in the wild desert places. Then the different tribes slowly settled into Canaan, in the land we call Palestine.

> **proph-et:**
> one who speaks for God.

At last, the prophet Samuel made Saul the first king. Later, it was King David who captured the city of Jerusalem and made it the center of religion and government.

The nation grew under David. The people saw success as another sign of God's special covenant. But after the reign of David's son, Solomon, the kingdom was divided into two parts, north and south. Ten tribes broke away to form the Northern Kingdom called Israel. Only the territory of the two tribes of Benjamin and Judah remained loyal to the king in Jerusalem. This Southern Kingdom was named Judah. It lasted long after the rival Northern Kingdom disappeared from history.

The Witness of the Prophets

After the nation was divided into two parts, an unusual group of religious leaders—the Hebrew prophets—appeared in Israel and Judah. They began to speak on behalf of God. The Hebrew prophets called attention to the wrong ways of the people. They said that the covenant required the nation to seek mercy and provide justice for all.

Amos told the people of Israel that God wanted justice in their courts and fair play in their business life.

The people of Israel thought that God would always protect them. They thought, "Isn't that what the covenant means?"

They looked forward to "the Day of the Lord" as a time when God would take their side in history to make the covenant promises come true.

The prophet Amos told them they were mistaken. God held them responsible.

Amos said that "the Day of the Lord" was actually the time when God would judge his people.

According to the prophet Amos, God had no "pet" people. The people of Israel were "special" to God because he had given them a big responsibility: to teach others how to live justly and mercifully.

Read Amos 7:10-17.
- What was Amos accused of doing?
- What answer did Amos give?

HOSEA presented God's case against Israel

Hosea called the prophet God's watchman, placed on the alert to look after the people.
- Hosea : 9:8

Hosea said that God wanted what was right and fair in society and government.

Hosea condemned the false oaths, the robberies, the killings.
- 4:2

Hosea condemned the sacrifices to pagan idols.
- 4:13

Hosea said that God wanted justice: "It will come to us like a shower, like spring rains that water the earth.
- 6:3 (NEB)

Hosea said that God would forgive Israel. "They shall return and dwell beneath my shadow, they shall flourish as a garden." -14:7

Hosea told of God, who was like a father helping his little son learn how to walk. "When Israel was a child, I loved him, and out of Egypt called my son."
- 11:1

Read Hosea 4:1-3.

• What was the cause of God's quarrel with Israel?

Read Hosea 11:1-4.

• How is God described?

The people did not listen to the prophet's warnings—Israel was destroyed by the Assyrians in 722 B.C.

The Southern Kingdom of Judah also had prophets.

ISAIAH was commissioned in the temple.

—6:1-8

He taught that all nations would come to the mountain of the Lord.

—2:2

He told of the day when swords would be beaten into plowshares, and spears into hooks used to prune fruit trees.

—2:4

Isaiah spoke of a faithful servant who was willing to suffer to be a good servant to others.

This idea of the "suffering servant" meant that the people of God were to be servants for the good of all people.

Isaiah said that God was unhappy with their religious events: "...sacred seasons and ceremonies, I cannot endure. I cannot tolerate... your festivals." —1:13-14 (NEB)

Isaiah is remembered for his promise of God's care for his people. God would send a future King to govern them with fairness and justice.

"for a boy has been born for us, a son given to us...." —9:6 (NE

Read Isaiah 1:13, 17.
- What does Isaiah say that God really wants?
- What must the people do to satisfy God?

JEREMIAH

blamed the people for burning sacrifices to idols.
—1:16

The prophet accused the leaders of the people of turning against God.

Because of the evil ways of the people, their cities would be destroyed. —4:20

Jeremiah condemned the powerful for not paying attention to the needs of orphans
—5:28

Nor did they grant justice to the poor.

Jeremiah reminded the people that God had rescued them when they were prisoners in Egypt.
—31:32

The old law had been carved on tablets of stone.

The new law would be within the people—written on their hearts.

Read Jeremiah 31:31-34.
- What was the old covenant?
- What is the new covenant, according to Jeremiah?
- What does it mean that the covenant will be written upon the people's hearts?

The prophets tried to tell the people what would go wrong if they didn't pay attention to God.

The nation ignored the warnings of the prophets.

Judah was defeated. Her citizens were captured and taken away into exile in Babylonia

Ex-ile: to be taken away by force from one's native land as a prisoner, to a strange land.

The exiles had lost Jerusalem and were without a king.

Their temple was gone and they had no priests.

WHAT COULD THEY DO ?

The captives were allowed to gather and pray.

They thought and talked about their problems.

EZEKIEL helped them to see that they deserved their punishment.

Ezekiel told them that God had kept his part of the covenant.

But they, the people, had not kept their part.

The Exile was a time for thinking about what had gone wrong.

Ezekiel helped them understand that God was using hard times to set things right among his pe.

This is a time-line. It shows the dates of the early fathers, some of the kings, and the prophets. Can you find the date when the nation of Israel was divided?

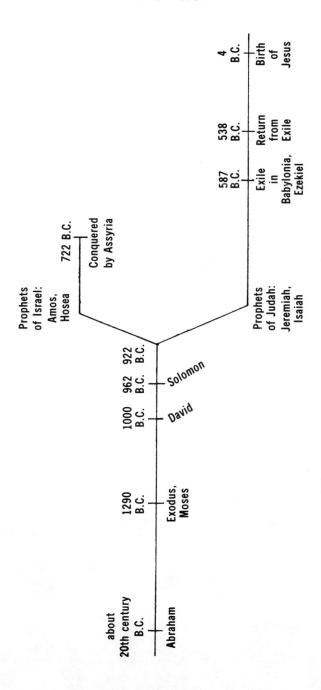

Four important religious customs started while the people were in exile. Out of their experience, the Jews began
to keep the sabbath faithfully,
to gather in synagogues,
to study the Scripture, and
to obey the Law strictly.
These religious customs and practices were the religion of Jesus, the disciples, and early Christian leaders, such as Paul of Tarsus.

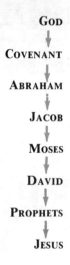

The covenant began between Abraham and God. It was carried on through many leaders, including the prophets. Early Christians were sure that what the prophets had promised actually came true in Jesus Christ. Jesus lived his life the way God wanted persons to live.

Jesus began his work as a religious teacher in Galilee. He later led his small group of disciples to Jerusalem.

In his teaching Jesus used the lessons he learned from studying the prophets.

Amos preached of "the day of the Lord" as a time when God would judge his people . . .

Jesus taught about a day when God's kingdom would actually come into human history.

Hosea told of God's love and kindness . . .

Jesus talked about God as a loving father. Because of Jesus, we begin our prayers with "Our Father."

Isaiah told of a suffering servant . . .

Jesus knelt and washed the feet of his disciples, the way a slave might do it.

Jeremiah told of the new covenant . . .

When Jesus shared the bread and the common cup for the last time with his closest friends, he said:
"This cup . . . is the new covenant" (Luke 22:20).
Jesus was saying that his followers were to commit themselves from their hearts out of love instead of doing it just because of the rules.

The New Testament begins with the good news of Jesus' work. Four different writers tell what Jesus taught and did. They are Matthew, Mark, Luke, and John. The book of Acts tells how a new community—the Christian church—was formed. The life of the Christian community is also described in the letters of Paul. The Bible is the history of God's special relationship with people. The community of faith celebrates God's activities among people.

Some Things for You to Do:

1. Pretend that you are one of the prophets. Pretend that you are "in his shoes" or "in his skin." Try to think as he would think. Spend several days looking at newspapers and magazines. Cut out all the titles, articles, or pictures about conditions the prophet would speak against if he were here today. Place them on a chart or poster.

   Or,

   Watch TV or listen to radio news reports. Jot down notes about conditions today about which the prophet might speak.

2. Think about the message of Jesus. What are the ways it is being carried out in society today? Cut out pictures or news captions that illustrate how the message is being demonstrated in your church and community. Make a poster of these.

3
Joining the Community of Faith

What does the word "community" mean to you? What does it remind you of?

Community can mean many things—

persons living together,
persons counting on each other,
persons sharing together in good times and hard times,
persons caring for one another,
persons helping one another.

> **com-mu-ni-ty:**
> a group of persons with a common interest.

This chapter is about the community of faith. Christians have joined together since the time of Christ two thousand years ago. Those who follow Christ commit themselves to a fellowship called the church. In the following pages you will find out how the church is a community of faith. You will also discover the special place Baptists have within the Christian community.

COMMUNITY
COMMITMENT

Some Things to Think About:

Why are there different churches?
How are Baptists related to the Christians of the Bible?
How are Baptists like other Christians today?
What is special about the Baptists?

A Community of Faith Around the World

To make the decision to follow Jesus usually means to join a congregation. A congregation is a group of "deciders for Jesus." They gather together to help one another live in a Christian way. Not all the disciples will be your age, or your sex, or your skin color, or your nationality. The people of God are of many different ages and backgrounds.

> **con-gre-ga-tion:** a religious community; a gathering of persons for worship and religious instruction.

Who is the oldest Christian you know? The youngest? There are Christian congregations in small towns and large cities. They are in very old cities and in very new places, just being built. Let your mind sweep across

your town,

your state, your nation,

your world.

Did you know . . .

• You can find Christian congregations on these continents:

> **North America**
>
> **Europe**
>
> **South America** **Asia**
>
> **Africa**
>
> **Australia**

• Christian people are to be found in all races of mankind. Some famous Christians are:

D. T. Niles

Martin Luther King, Jr.

Corita Kent

Religious News Service

Wide World Photos

Courtesy of Chinese Cultural and Community Center of Philadelphia

Sun Yat Sen

When you join a congregation, you become a part of a larger community of faith around the world. It is often called an ecumenical fellowship. It is pronounced eck-you-men-ick-ul.

> **ec-u-men-i-cal:**
> worldwide; representing
> churches from all around
> the world; Christians from
> all the earth working to-
> gether.

Many words in English began as words in another language. Ecumenical is a word that comes from the Greek word *Oikos*, which means house. Ecumenical means the household of faith that includes people from many different Christian groups. It is a way of saying "We are one big family because of Jesus Christ." Your own congregation may belong to a larger ecumenical fellowship in your town or city.

How many different churches are there where you live? Check this list and add others you may find:

Assembly of God	Church of God
American Baptist	United Church of Christ
Seventh-Day Adventist	United Methodist
Seventh-Day Baptist	United Presbyterian
Southern Baptist	United Lutheran
Church of the Nazarene	American Lutheran
Disciples of Christ	Roman Catholic

Why Are There Different Churches?

Why are there so many congregations? So many different churches?

It all began in the centuries immediately after the time of Christ. Following the New Testament times, Christians moved into every part of Europe and Asia Minor.

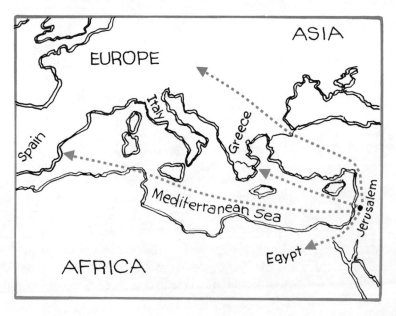

Jesus' words to the apostles in Acts 1:8 were: "But you will be filled with power when the Holy Spirit comes on you, and you will be witnesses for me in Jerusalem, in all of Judea and Samaria, and to the ends of the earth" (TEV).

The first big split between Christians took place because the Roman Empire was so big. One of the emperors divided it into two parts. He shared the task of governing with another ruler. In time, the differences between the two halves of the Empire made two different churches. There were differences in language and customs. A number of churches claimed a connection with one of Jesus' disciples (or apostles, as they came to be called).

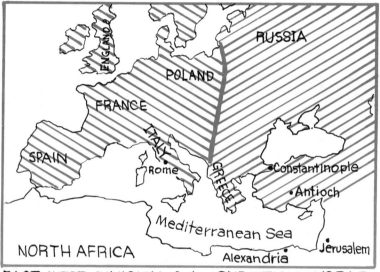

EAST-WEST DIVISION of the CHRISTIAN WORLD
\\\\\ =Western Christianity ///=Eastern Christianity

The churches founded in the East by the apostles included those in Jerusalem, Antioch, Constantinople, and Alexandria. The only church founded in the West by the apostles was in Rome. This made for a different history of Christianity in the West. The Eastern churches always shared in the leadership. The Christians in the West had only one leading church for over a thousand years.

The following chart shows some other differences:

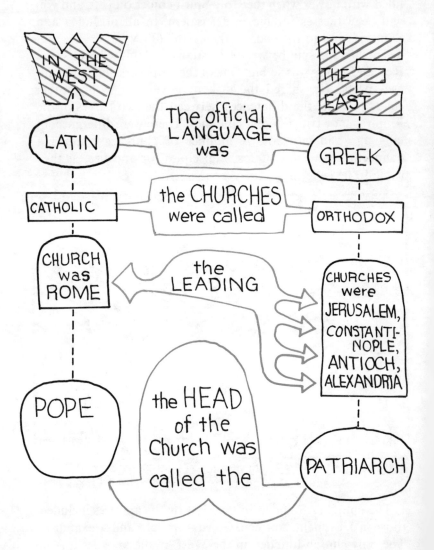

The Reform Movement

There was only one church in Western Europe for over a thousand years—the Catholic Church. (The word "catholic" itself means universal or "existing everywhere.") Then in the sixteenth century, people became unhappy with the Church. Many leaders felt it was not following Christianity as it is found in the New Testament. They began a movement to reform (or make over) the Church. Such persons as Martin Luther, John Calvin, and Menno Simons were leaders in the Reform Movement, or Reformation, as it is often called. The Reform Movement finally caused a split in the Catholic Church. From that split we have the Protestant and Catholic groups as we know them today.

. . . in Europe

The following chart shows how those who wanted to make over the Catholic Church in continental Europe caused different church groups to form. The persons who wanted change ranged from those listed on the left side, who wanted radical or big changes, to those on the right side, who wanted few or small changes.

Reformation in Europe

**Those who
wanted radical or big changes**

**Those who
wanted few
or small changes**

Rome

Leader: Martin Luther
Followers were called: Lutherans.
Today they are called: Lutherans.

Leader: John Calvin
Followers were called: the Reformed Church.
Today they are called: Presbyterians
(some are also called Reform).

Leader: Menno Simons
Followers were called: Anabaptists.
Today they are called: Mennonites.

. . . in England

The Reformation in England grew differently from the Reformation in the rest of Europe. In England, the Reform Movement brought about the Church of England, or the Anglican Church. Many English reformers still wanted more changes in even the Anglican Church. The Puritans worked for reform within the Anglican Church. Another group, the Separatists, separated from the church entirely. Puritans may be familiar to you. These were the pilgrims who founded the settlements of Plymouth, Salem, and Boston in Massachusetts. Some of the Puritans and Separatists became Presbyterians and Congregationalists. Baptists also came from England, and their history began in the seventeenth century.

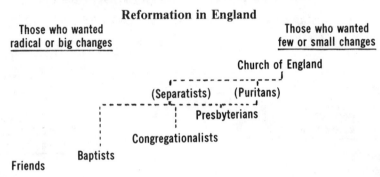

Reformation in England

Those who wanted radical or big changes

Those who wanted few or small changes

Church of England

(Separatists)   (Puritans)

Presbyterians

Congregationalists

Baptists

Friends

The left-hand column of the chart on the next page may help you to see what all Christians share in common. The middle column shows what many Protestant churches believe. The right-hand column describes the key ideas contributed by early Baptists.

Some Things for You to Do:

1. Find out how other churches are like or different from your church. Have you ever wondered how other churches in your neighborhood differ from yours? Sometimes it is interesting to compare the practices of your congregation with those of others. Begin with how your congregation admits persons into the fellowship.

- What does a person do who wants to be baptized and become a member of the church?
- How is baptism carried out?
- At what age?
- Under whose direction?

BELIEFS SHARED BY ALL CHRISTIANS Orthodox, Catholic, and Protestant	THE PROTESTANT REFORMATION EMPHASIZED	RELIGIOUS IDEAS BAPTISTS CONTRIBUTED
↓	↓	↓

THE INCARNATION

Jesus was God's Son, present on earth in human flesh.
Read Philippians 2:5-11.

SALVATION BY FAITH

The Christian can be saved by simply accepting God's gift.
Read Galatians 3:26-29.

FREEDOM OF CONSCIENCE

Every person is responsible to God and free to respond in an individual way.
Read Galatians 5:1.

THE LIFE AND MINISTRY OF JESUS

The good news of Jesus' life and work on earth is the main message of the Christian church.
Read Mark 1:14-39.

THE PLACE OF THE BIBLE

The Old and New Testaments are the key to understanding how God wants people to live and behave.
Read 1 Timothy 4:13.

RELIGIOUS LIBERTY

Persons and groups have the right to worship and live before God in their own way.
Read Romans 14:10-12.

THE GIFT OF THE SPIRIT

The living Spirit of Christ is present with the people who follow him today.
Read Romans 5:5.

THE PRIESTHOOD OF BELIEVERS

Every Christian is called to be a minister to others and to minister to any neighbor's needs.
Read 1 Corinthians 12:4-7; Romans 12: 4-5.

THE SEPARATION OF CHURCH AND STATE

Individuals are not to be forced into a pattern set by any "official state church."
Read Mark 12:13-17.

BELIEVER'S BAPTISM

The church is made up of those able to make up their own minds about belonging to the church.
Read Acts 18:8.

CHRIST, OUR REDEMPTION

Jesus has saved all humanity from the bad ending caused by sin and evil.
Read Colossians 1:22.

2. Compare the practice of your church with another Protestant church—Episcopal, Presbyterian, or other.
   - Does baptism take place? If so, when?
   - When does a person become a church member?
   - What is the special occasion of becoming a church member called?
3. Find out about a Roman Catholic church.
   - At what age is baptism?
   - What does baptism mean for the person?
   - At what age does a person become a member?
   - What is required of a person for formal membership?
4. Find out about a Jewish congregation.
   - At what age does a person become a member of a synagogue?
   - What is a *Bar Mitzvah?*
   - What is a *Bas Mitzvah?*
   - What is required of a Jewish young person before he or she may become a member of the Jewish synagogue?

Some ways to help you carry on your research:

1. Read books and encyclopedias that your church, school, or public library may have, such as

One God: The Ways We Worship Him, by Florence M. Fitch.

The New Catholic Encyclopedia

Encyclopedia Judaica

2. Arrange to interview a minister of a Methodist, Episcopal, or Presbyterian church. Or, if you prefer, interview the priest of a local Catholic parish or the rabbi or a local or nearby Jewish synagogue. Before the interview think about the questions you want to ask; then telephone the church office and arrange an appointment. Take along a cassette tape recorder to record the conversation.

3. Arrange to visit a Catholic church to observe a confirmation service, or a Jewish synagogue to observe a *Bar Mitzvah* ceremony.

4. Talk with your friends who belong to different churches and get their ideas and beliefs.

4
Learning About the Baptist Heritage

Baptist men and women through the centuries have stood up for their beliefs. Many have contributed new ideas to what it means to be a Christian. This chapter will look at the freedom fighters in Baptist history. You may discover how they influenced what you believe today.

Some Things to Think About:

Who are some of the great Baptists in history?
How were they different?
What did they contribute to mankind?
How are their ideas important to us today?

Freedom Fighters in Our Past

Study the lives of these Baptist pioneers, and
   discover WHY they were freedom fighters.
After reading the histories of these Baptist freedom fighters, think about how we follow their ideas in our churches and in our communities.
These Baptist pioneers put their faith to work.
Read Galatians 5:1.
   • Describe what the gospel says about liberty.
   • How did the Baptist pioneers follow this verse?
   • How do we take this verse seriously today?

Lott Cary
About 1780-1828

Lott Cary was born a slave. Being a slave meant working without pay. Children were often taken from their families to work another farm.

He was very unhappy. In order to forget his miserable life, he began to drink liquor. Lott was drunk a great deal of the time. At the age of 27, Cary became a believer and joined the First Baptist Church of Richmond, Virginia. God helped him to change his life. He stopped drinking and began to tell others about Jesus.

Lott learned how to read. He began reading the Bible. In time, he was able to buy his freedom for $850, a lot of money.

Cary got people interested in telling Africans about Jesus. Both black and white people gave money and prayed for God's help.

In 1821 the Baptist General Convention chose Lott Cary as their missionary. He sailed to Africa in 1821 and finally settled in Liberia, West Africa, in 1822. He is remembered as the first American to go to Africa as a missionary.

Walter Rauschenbusch, 1861–1918

In the 1800s and early 1900s the United States grew rapidly. People came from Europe. The cities grew. Railroads were built.

Walter Rauschenbusch, a German Baptist minister, cared for the suffering people crowded into the big cities.

Rauschenbusch worked in New York City's "Hell's Kitchen."

A preacher of the gospel, Rauschenbusch believed that the Good News of Jesus had something to say about how people lived and worked.

Rauschenbusch taught that Christians must do something about crooked politics!

TAMMANY HALL

With other Christians Rauschenbusch fought for shorter working hours (eight hours a day), fewer work days (to allow for a forty-hour weekend), against the use of children as laborers in factories and mines, and for better working conditions for women.

He is famous for insisting that the heart of Jesus' message was "the kingdom of God on earth."

Walter Rauschenbusch is remembered in American history for helping to lead the way to a fairer, better life for common people.

Helen Barrett Montgomery
1861–1934

Helen Barrett Montgomery organized and taught a Bible class in Lake Avenue Baptist Church, Rochester, New York. She was the first woman member of the Rochester School Board. She also helped organize
—a dental clinic,
—an open air school for tubercular children, and
—the first factory school in the nation.

She was the first president of the Women's Educational and Industrial Union of Rochester. She sponsored
—a legal aid center,
—the first public playground,
—milk stations for needy mothers (which became child welfare clinics), and
—a social settlement.

In 1913 she was invited to travel around the world to study mission fields. She wrote The King's Highway, a best-seller. She also translated the Greek New Testament into modern English (The Centenary Translation of the New Testament, 1924).

She served as president of the Woman's American Baptist Foreign Mission Society, 1914–1924.

She worked to open the University of Rochester to women. In 1921 she was elected president of the Northern Baptist Convention. Helen Barrett Montgomery was the first woman to hold such a high position in any large Christian church or denomination.

In her lifetime she received honorary degrees from Brown University, Franklin College, Denison University, and Wellesley.

Charles Evans Hughes
1862-1948

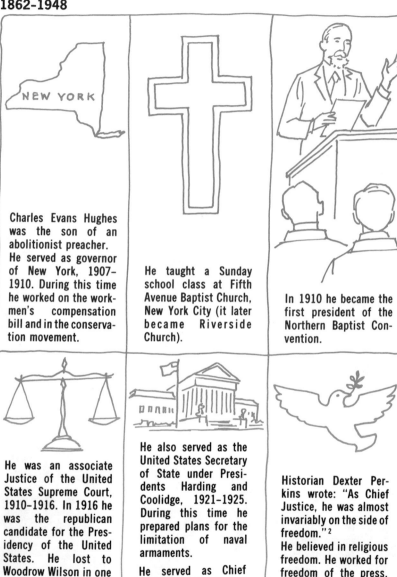

Charles Evans Hughes was the son of an abolitionist preacher. He served as governor of New York, 1907–1910. During this time he worked on the workmen's compensation bill and in the conservation movement.

He taught a Sunday school class at Fifth Avenue Baptist Church, New York City (it later became Riverside Church).

In 1910 he became the first president of the Northern Baptist Convention.

He was an associate Justice of the United States Supreme Court, 1910–1916. In 1916 he was the republican candidate for the Presidency of the United States. He lost to Woodrow Wilson in one of the closest elections in United States history.

He also served as the United States Secretary of State under Presidents Harding and Coolidge, 1921–1925. During this time he prepared plans for the limitation of naval armaments.

He served as Chief Justice of the United States Supreme Court, 1930–1941.

Historian Dexter Perkins wrote: "As Chief Justice, he was almost invariably on the side of freedom." [2]
He believed in religious freedom. He worked for freedom of the press, the place of labor in a democratic society, and civil rights.

[2] Dexter Perkins, *Charles Evans Hughes and American Democratic Statesmanship,* ed. Oscar Handlin (Boston: Little, Brown and Company, 1956), p. 165.

Elizabeth Garland Hall
1867–1933

Elizabeth Garland Hall was born in Augusta, Maine. Her parents died when she was an infant. She became the ward of a Boston lady of Christian culture and refinement.

At a very early age, she wanted to become a missionary. At eighteen she went to the Chicago Baptist Training School to prepare for a missionary career.

Here she was to know prejudice. She was enrolled as "Elizabeth Garland, colored." She had been assured by her guardian that her parents were from Europe, near the Black Sea. Her life was changed by this knowledge of her heritage.

Elizabeth was assigned a paper on Africa. It was then that she decided to go to Africa. She met and married William A. Hall, a missionary from Jamaica. In Africa she worked very hard, ministering to all sorts of needs. She was called "Mama Hall."

In Africa Elizabeth contracted black water fever four times and could no longer serve the people she had learned to love.

She went to her island home in Jamaica, which was almost as primitive as her African home. Because of her great contributions to the Jamaicans, she was again called "Mama Hall."

When a dread disease broke out, "Mama Hall" isolated the victims, and for twenty-one months she nursed and cared for them with only the help of one or two unwilling helpers whom she had to train.

She is best known for her "Pansy Garden," a home for little children, for which she used her own small bungalow. She taught them many things, including Bible study, to improve their lives. Her health gave out, and she had to come home to the United States, where she died about a year later.

Martin Luther King, Jr.,
civil rights leader, 1929-1968

Martin Luther King, Jr. graduated from Morehouse College, Crozer Theological Seminary, and Boston University.

He was intensely interested in Gandhi and the style of nonviolent disobedience to unjust laws.

He was pastor of the Dexter Street Baptist Church, Montgomery, Alabama, 1954–1960. Also, he led the Montgomery bus boycott. He helped found the Southern Christian Leadership Conference, an early nonviolent movement for civil rights.

A highlight of his life came when he was awarded the Nobel Peace Prize in 1964. When he received this prize, he said, ". . . nonviolence is the answer to the crucial political and racial questions of our time. . . ."[3]

Oslo, Norway,
December 10, 1964

He wrote "Letter from Birmingham Jail" and several books.

His life was threatened many times. On April 4, 1968, he died a martyr's death in Memphis, Tennessee. He had gone there to help garbage collectors, black and white, earn a salary large enough for their living needs.

[3]Coretta Scott King, *My Life with Martin Luther King, Jr.* (New York: Avon Books, 1969), p. 26.

Some Things for You to Do:

1. Illustrate the contributions of these Baptist pioneers.
   - *Poster*—Choose one or more of the Baptist pioneers. Put on the poster pictures from magazines or those you draw yourself which illustrate their special contributions.
   - *Montage*—Select pictures from magazines and include your own artwork. Use headlines from newspapers that tell of religious liberty, freedom of conscience, civil rights, women's rights, and child welfare.

   Display the poster or montage on a bulletin board or tripod in your church.
2. Look for information on the following:
   - How Baptists are "freedom fighters" today.
   - What kinds of issues or social problems Baptists are concerned with today.

   Ways to do your research:
   1. Interview your pastor, parents, committee, or board members in your church responsible for missions.
   2. Read denominational magazines, either state or national ones.

5
Understanding the Life of My Church

Every community or congregation of Christians that tries to follow Jesus must organize its shared life. This chapter is about the Baptist congregation. It may help you know the life of your own Baptist church.

Some Things to Think About:

What does my church do?
What is the business of my church?
What are the special observances in my church?
What does it mean to belong to my church?

Baptists were known as church reformers. They used the New Testament church as their example. Baptists tried to organize their congregations according to what they read in the Acts of the Apostles. They also studied the first Christian letters that told about the earliest churches.

The first step in organizing a group was to choose a leader or leaders. The disciples had to make such choices.

Read Acts 1:15-26. This tells about an early event in church organization.

- What was the business of the meeting?
- Who acted as the leader?
- What did those gathered at the meeting have to do?
- How did they handle the problem?
- What decisions did they make?

The early church grew. Their work increased. They soon found a new problem in organization.

Read Acts 6:1-7.

- What was the problem?
- Who called the meeting?
- What was the group asked to do?
- How did the group act?

The New Testament church believed *all* the members of the Christian community were important. It believed that all Christ's followers were responsible for the Christian ministry. *Read* 1 Corinthians 12:27-30.

- How do these verses describe the Christian community?

For centuries, Baptist congregations have organized according to the example of the early church. All members share in the work of the church. They choose their leaders. Just as Jesus helped others, every member is responsible to serve as a minister.

What is the work of the Christian community? What does it do? The New Testament makes it clear that Christians do not work alone. The followers of Christ work together as members of one body. Read 1 Corinthians 12:27 again.

What Is Basic to the Christian Ministry of Baptists?

In 2 Corinthians 5:19, Paul, the early Christian missionary, described God's mission as "reconciliation." The work of Baptists is to increase reconciliation between persons. This ministry is based upon God's reconciling work as Jesus practiced it. What examples of reconciliation come to your mind?

... Think of a time when you and your parents worked out some problem, after which all of you felt better.

... Can you recall a quarrel with a friend? How did you work it out? Did you find a way to make up?

> rec-on-cil-i-a-tion: to restore to friendship and to bring into harmony; includes the settling of differences.

. . . Do you remember seeing two people on opposite sides of an argument? Can you recall their finding some way to settle their differences?

Reconciliation means rebuilding good relations between persons. To be "in Christ" includes being connected to other persons in a trusting, accepting way.

How My Local Congregation Organizes for Its Christian Mission

Every Baptist congregation is different. This section is about your own church and how it is organized. The information to be filled in can only be found in your own congregation. You may need to ask your pastor, church officers, parents, or other adult leaders to help you find the necessary information.

Every congregation organizes to meet certain needs.
1. It needs to have a place
   for study,
       for worship, and
           other gatherings and activities;
   so the congregation
       constructs a building,
           heats and cools the rooms, and
               provides lighting.

In many churches, a *board of trustees* is responsible for the building. Who in your church is responsible for the building?

2. A congregation needs to provide for worship.
   Needed are
       —a place to gather for worship;
       —music and hymnbooks for the congregation, as well as music for the choir;
       —a musical instrument to accompany the congregation as they sing, such as an organ or piano;
       —a person to lead the worship.

A *board of deacons* is responsible for worship in many Baptist churches. Who is responsible for worship in your congregation?

3. A congregation needs to provide for spiritual leadership
    —to help in the study of the Scriptures,
    —to teach God's good news as shown in Jesus Christ,
    —to help persons develop a devotional life,
    —to help call on the sick and shut-in, and
    —to help organize the work of the congregation.

A minister is often the spiritual leader of a congregation. In Baptist churches the members of the congregation call a minister. "To call" means to invite a person to be the leader. A congregation is careful to select a person who has special education for the work of the ministry.

All members of the Christian community are to serve in the Christian ministry. Ministers—or members of the clergy, as they are called—are trained to help all members do the work of the church. This follows the example given in Ephesians 4:12. Different persons are given different talents in order "to prepare all God's people for the work of Christian service, to build up the body of Christ" (TEV).

How do the members of your congregation share in the ministry? How does the leader of your congregation help its members to serve in a Christian ministry?

4. A congregation needs to provide for Christian teaching. It wants to help persons live in a Christian way.
    It needs
    —Bibles to study;
    —church school teachers to help lead the study of Scripture and other learning materials;

—church school resources, such as maps, dictionaries, commentaries on the Bible, films, records, etc.

What is the committee or board in your church that plans Christian education? How does it plan Christian education?

5. A congregation usually wants to carry the good news of God in Christ into all the world. The congregation needs to
   —provide information on how mission is carried out both overseas and here at home;
   —support the work of "international workers" for Christ. These persons are often called missionaries;
   —support the work of the larger group of Baptists—the denomination—in its international and national mission work.

How does your congregation organize for missionary work?

6. Many congregations find it helpful to organize groups to provide for the needs of persons.

   People need to get together for special

   tasks

   or

   just for fun and fellowship!

   What are some of these groups in your congregation? Give specific names of the groups and identify the present leaders.

   Women's groups:

   Youth groups:

   Organized church school classes:

   Organized activities:

How My Congregation Celebrates Its Life Together

Congregational Worship

At the center of the life of every congregation is the worship of God. Members of the church gather together
to praise God,
to give thanks,
to confess their need for God's
power in their lives, and
to ask for strength and wisdom
to live in the Christian way!

Baptist Ordinances

Baptists refer to the acts of baptism and the Lord's Supper as ordinances. Christ ordained these two to be carried out by his followers.

Both baptism and the Lord's Supper are found in the New Testament. They are honored in some way by all Christian churches.

> **or-dain:**
> **to appoint or assign a special purpose to.**
> **or-di-nance:**
> **a practice or ceremony suggested or given by an authority.**

BAPTISM

In Acts 2:14-42, there is an account of Peter's sermon on the day of Pentecost.

> Pentecost was a Jewish religious festival celebrated fifty days after the Passover. Pentecost became the birthday of the Christian church when the people at a festival gathering became aware of and filled with the Holy Spirit. See Acts 2:1-4.

Peter's sermon is a good example of the first preaching of the earliest Christian community. Peter presented the good news so convincingly that the people gathered around him asked,

"What shall we do?" Read Acts 2:38 to find out what Peter recommended.

What did Peter say that baptism would do for his listeners?

Chapter nine of Acts describes the conversion of Saul. He was an early persecutor of Christians. Saul was a kind of religious "bounty-hunter." To find out where his persecution of the church ended, read Acts 9:1-30.

What do you think baptism meant to Saul? (Acts 9:17-19)

What new name was given to Saul? (Acts 13:9)

There are many places in the New Testament where baptism is mentioned. It was an important religious practice in the life of the first Christians. So it is not surprising to find early Christian thinkers writing about its meaning.

In Romans 6:3-4, Paul—the Saul who was converted in Acts 9—describes baptism. He says it is the Christian taking part in Christ's death (burial in the baptismal waters) and resurrection (rising in the new being of a Christian).

THE LORD'S SUPPER

The central part of worship for all Christians is the Lord's Supper. Both the priest in the Catholic mass and the leader in the more simple Baptist observance of the Lord's Supper repeat the same words:

> For I received from the Lord what I also delivered to you, that the Lord Jesus on the night when he was betrayed took bread, and when he had given thanks, he broke it, and said, "This is my body which is for you. Do this in remembrance of me." In the same way also the cup, after supper, saying, "This cup is the new covenant in my blood. Do this, as often as you drink it, in remembrance of me." For as often as you eat this bread and drink the cup, you proclaim the Lord's death until he comes.
>
> *1 Corinthians 11:23-26*

Jesus shared a common meal with his disciples for the final time. He took the bread and the cup that was a regular part of their meals. He gave these ordinary things a special meaning.

The Lord's Supper celebrates the memory of the last time Jesus was with his disciples before his crucifixion (see 1 Corinthians 11:25). The Lord's Supper is also a present experience. It is celebrated today when we as his disciples share bread and drink together and recall Jesus' words. Also, it looks toward the future. In 1 Corinthians 11:26 Jesus' words make the Lord's Supper a promise of what is still to come.

The Lord's Supper celebrates:

the past—as a memorial,

the present—as the sharing of the Scriptures and the elements of life, food and drink,

the future—as looking forward to reunion with the Lord.

These three elements are part of the religious observance started by Jesus himself.

My Congregation Is Part of a Worldwide Church

The congregation of which you will be an important part is itself part of a larger fellowship. Your congregation belongs to a fellowship of churches usually referred to as a denomination.

Write out the name of your denomination.

What is the name of the state or regional group through which your congregation works?

Write down the address of the national headquarters of your national church organization.

You will notice that there are other Christian denominations besides the one you are joining. Perhaps you remember the word *ecumenical.* It refers to the many churches of different denominations that join together. The purpose of the ecumenical movement is to work together. As a team, the members put aside their differences. They bring their strengths together to carry out a better ministry.

Many Christian denominations today work together in hospitals,
> schools,
>> publishing houses, and
>>> missions around the world.

What is the name of the local ecumenical group with which your church cooperates?

Through what international group does your local congregation work?

List some examples of work done by ecumenical cooperation.

Some Things for You to Do:

1. Interviews: Interview some of the older members of your congregation. They may tell you information you could not find elsewhere. Be sure to make an appointment ahead of the meeting. It helps if people know why you are interviewing them. Share your reason: this interview is part of your preparation for church membership. Tape your interview. Think ahead about the questions you may ask; you could ask questions such as:
   - How long have you been a member of this congregation?
   - For what would you like our congregation to be remembered?
   - What different kinds of services or ministries has our congregation provided?
   - What changes have you seen take place through the years?
   - What has changed the most? The least?

(Note: If you tape an interview, you may wish to send a copy of your tape to the American Baptist Historical Society, 1120

South Goodman Street, Rochester, NY 14620. If you wish to do this, carefully give the dates, the name of the person(s) you interviewed, the place of the interview, the full name of the local congregation of which you are a part, and the city and state in which it is located. Tapes, carefully made with full details, can be helpful in creating an oral history collection.)

2. What's in a cornerstone? When a church building is erected, many times historical items are placed in the cornerstone. It's interesting to know what is in such cornerstones, and, without opening them, it is sometimes possible to discover the contents.

- Get the date of the cornerstone-laying ceremony from the cornerstone itself.
- Ask the church clerk to help you find the church minutes for that date. These minutes may tell you the contents of the receptacle which was placed in the cornerstone.
- Or, look up the newspaper published in your city or neighborhood for that date. Newspaper files are usually located in the office of the newspaper (if it's still published), public libraries, or historical societies. Newspaper articles describing such laying ceremonies often list the items secured in the cornerstone.
- Or, ask some senior members of the congregation for information. They may have souvenirs of such cornerstone-laying ceremonies.

3. Comparison Time Line: Compare the history of your local congregation with what was happening in the nation and around the world.

   Make two parallel columns. In one column, list the names and dates of major historical events or personalities. (Pick a starting date near the time of the founding of your congregation.) In the other column, list the events that happened in the life of your congregation at about the same time. The following is an example of how a comparison time line may be done.

World/National Events	Events in the Life of My Congregation	
Lewis and Clark's Expedition (1804-1806)	The founding of the congregation	(date)
Charles Darwin's **Origin of Species** (1859)	The building of the church	(date)
The American Civil War (1861-1865)	Pastors of the church	(dates)
The Great War in Europe, World War I (1914-1918)	Youth events at the church	(dates)
Revolution in Russia (1917)	Special choir events	(dates)
Women's Suffrage (19th Amendment, 1920)	Special women's events	(dates)
The Great Depression (1930s)		
The Second World War (1939-1945)		
The Founding of the United Nations (1945)		
Man Lands on the Moon (1969)		

4. Edit a newspaper: You may wish to publish a newspaper about your congregation.
   - Report on activities of your members. Tell how they serve people day by day. Tell the story of how concerned Christians are caring for the special needs of people.
   - Relate interesting stories or happenings in families.
   - Interview persons.
   - Include cartoons that tell interesting facts about your church.
5. Publish a "Paper from the Past": Describe the early days of your congregation.
   - Use headlines announcing special events that happened.
   - Interview the oldest members and tell their stories.
   - Sketch pictures of the first church building.

- Sketch other changes in the building that took place throughout the years.
- List the first twenty-five members of the congregation.
- List the names of relatives of those first members who are still in the church.
6. Prepare a historical display: Research the history of your congregation's past. Prepare to display the history in wall posters or a wall mural. Gather together old photographs or church programs from senior members or the church clerk, and arrange them in a display.

6
Being
a Disciple

In this book you have been reading about the people of God and their lives in the organized church. You may have discovered how your own congregation learns together, worships together, and organizes for Christian mission. This chapter is about the role of the people of God beyond the church.

Some Things to Think About:

What does the ministry of Jesus mean to us today?
How can the church make a difference in the world?
What can the church do for peace and justice today?

Commitment to the discipleship of Jesus goes beyond the church. It requires

> *awareness* of what is happening outside the gathered Christian community of the church
> and
> *responsibility* for our neighbors in the world in which we live.

Who Is My Neighbor?

The following are three case studies. They may guide your understanding about what "neighbor" means to the Christian.

> **case stud-y:**
> a report about a situation to help us understand a similar situation in our lives.

The Parable of the Good Samaritan (from TEV)

A certain teacher of the Law came up and tried to trap Jesus. "Teacher," he asked, "what must I do to receive eternal life?"

Jesus answered him, "What do the Scriptures say? How do you interpret them?"

The man answered, "'You must love the Lord your God . . . with all your strength, and with all your mind'; and, 'You must love your fellow-man as yourself.'"

"Your answer is correct," replied Jesus; "do this and you will live."

But the teacher of the Law wanted to put himself in the right, so he asked Jesus, "Who is my fellow-man?"

Jesus answered, "There was a man who was going down from Jerusalem to Jericho, when robbers attacked him, stripped him, and beat him up, leaving him half dead. It so happened that a priest was going down that road; when he saw the man he walked on by, on the other side. In the same way a Levite also came there, went over and looked at the man, and then walked on by, on the other side. But a certain Samaritan who was traveling that way came upon him, and when he saw the man his heart was filled with pity. He went over to him, poured oil and wine on his wounds and bandaged them; then he put the man on his own animal and took him to an inn, where he took care of him. The next day he took out two silver coins and gave them to the innkeeper. 'Take care of him,' he told the innkeeper, 'and when I come back this way I will pay you back whatever you spend on him.'"

And Jesus concluded, "In your opinion, which one of these three acted like a fellow-man toward the man attacked by the robbers?"

The teacher of the Law answered, "The one who was kind to him."

Jesus replied, "You go, then, and do the same" (Luke 10:25-37, TEV).

- How does Jesus answer the lawyer?
- What is required in "loving one's neighbor (fellow-man)"?

A Good Samaritan Among the Migrants

Mexican-American families follow the harvesting of crops on the West Coast year after year. In Oregon, they pick the berries, beans, and nuts. Often the cars they own become their only permanent homes. When migrants stop in a town to pick crops, they are forced to live in whatever housing they find. Sometimes these people have many needs; they are often without proper clothing, food, or medical care. Because they move so often, their children are in and out of different schools. They are not able to keep up with schoolwork. The children often have difficulty with the basic subjects.

Letha Wakeman decided to help the migrants. She was a former missionary to Africa. She settled in a rural area where migrant families gathered. On her own she set up a mission to the migrant families in Eola Village, near McMinnville, Oregon. She held classes for young mothers. Mrs. Wakeman also taught the women to cook and sew. The mothers were then able to make quilts to keep their families warm. Letha Wakeman taught the children about Jesus Christ. Under her direction, worship services and Bible study were held in a small chapel. Later, a Spanish-speaking minister came to help.

Letha Wakeman never asked the local churches for funds to support her ministry. She did, however, tell the story of the needs of the migrants over and over again. People in the local community listened. Churches began to respond with gifts. The local Church Women United helped her work. Funds from different organizations were also given.

Clothing and food were collected through the influence of this missionary. Federal funds were solicited to provide tutors to help the children with their schoolwork. Letha Wakeman opened her small trailer home to the children. They were there every day, waiting for her stories and games. She often made cookies with them. They learned from her how to live as Christians.

When Letha Wakeman was seventy-five years old, the local Baptist church licensed her. This allowed her to marry young couples. She died in the summer of 1974. The county condemned the housing in Eola Village and made no plans to replace it. Without the influence of Letha Wakeman, there may be no further work with migrant families in that area.

- What is similar about this true story and the parable of the good Samaritan which Jesus told?
- How could the "people of God" in the town respond to the needs of the migrant people?

Leon Sullivan . . . "Opening the Opportunities"

People of minority groups have been discriminated against in the job market for many years. Few jobs have been available to them. Also, people of low income and minority groups have not been adequately prepared to take the jobs open to them.

In the late 1950s, Leon Sullivan, a black Baptist, began a ministry with young people in the slums of Philadelphia. Working with juvenile gangs, he organized a program to help youth find jobs.

In 1963, Dr. Sullivan, who was also minister of the Zion Baptist Church, started a unique job-training program. He rented an abandoned North Philadelphia police station and jail. The rent was one dollar a year. With the help of the church members and some industries in the Philadelphia area, the program grew. The U.S. Department of Labor recognized its value. The government contributed funds to the program. It became known all over the world. It was called the Opportunities Industrialization Centers (OIC). Leon Sullivan's idea has resulted in 110 centers in 43 states. It has been copied in six foreign countries.

Many people have been helped through these centers. In one of the OIC locations in New York City an abandoned bowling alley has been changed into brightly painted offices and classrooms. In this center people who have not finished high school learn bookkeeping and secretarial skills. Others learn basic electrical skills, while the center helps them complete their high school work.

At the request of a doctor in Nigeria, Dr. Sullivan traveled to Africa. He helped to set up OIC centers in Nigeria. He went on to set up other centers in Kenya, Ghana, and Ethiopia as well. In these centers people may. be trained for such jobs as commercial bakers, hotel staff workers, and auto mechanics.

People all over the world have benefited from the Opportunities Industrialization Centers' program. It all started with one man—Leon Sullivan. He was concerned enough about the lack of job training to work out a program. The centers help people to help themselves.

- How is this present-day program similar to Jesus' parable of the good Samaritan?

The two stories above are about actual people. The following story tells of something that just might have happened.

A City Neighborhood . . . a Possible Situation Today

Jess and his gang tossed the ball back and forth across the street—against the city buildings, above the storefronts, anywhere to make it difficult for the other team to get it. This was their own game, with some of the guys on one side of the street and some on the other.

"Get a load of that, will ya!" yelled Jess to the other guys. "A 'whitey' moving into our neighborhood! Someone gave them the wrong address—that's for sure! This street is for blacks only!"

"Man, can we ever give him a time!" shouted Jake. "Wow, a 'whitey' will really make the light glare on this street!"

"Yeah! Ha! Wait till we get him!" shouted one of the others in the gang.

- How is this story like the story of the good Samaritan?
- Who is the neighbor in this incident?
- How could one respond in a Christian way in this situation?

. . . We Are Called to Minister

The good Samaritan is a parable Jesus told. It shows the difference between his ministry and that of the other religious leaders of his day. The purpose of Jesus' ministry was not to be the great religious leader. Jesus wanted to help people in need.

The early disciples had three years with Jesus. They learned in real-life situations how Jesus understood his ministry. They learned while

the lepers were being touched,

Jesus was visiting the tax collectors, and

the hungry were being fed.

By looking closely at Jesus' ministry, you may discover the role of the people of God outside of the church.

Read how Jesus defined his ministry in Luke 4:16-21. What does Jesus' ministry mean to those who follow him today?

The Proclamation of Jesus

". . . to preach good news to the poor . . ."

then

now

What Does Jesus' Ministry Mean to Us Today?

". . . to preach good news to the poor . . ."

- What do the poor need?
- How are we responsible for providing adequate clothing, food, housing?
- What difference does this make in one's attitude toward the poor?

The Proclamation of Jesus

". . . proclaim release to the captives . . ."

then

now

Jean-Claude LeJeune

What Does Jesus' Ministry Mean to Us Today?

". . . proclaim release to the captives . . ."

- What are some ways people are captive today?
- Who are the captives?
- What happens when people's goals are directed by greed rather than by what happens to fellow humans?

The Proclamation of Jesus

". . . recovering of sight to the blind,"

then

now

Portugal Fears Coup, Alerts Armed Forces

GUN BATTLE RAGES IN CENTRAL BEIRUT

One Man Slain, 2d Shot in Holdup

Prices Up And So Is Inflation

Consumers Hit By Many Boosts

Missing Delco Girl Is Found Nearly Dead

Angolan militiamen wave their machetes as they join in a celebration of independence in Luanda

Two Governments Set Up; Angolan Strife Intensifies

5 Men Fire Shots

Darby Girl Slain In Father's Arms

Poll Shows Heavy Opposition to Racial Busing

What Does Jesus' Ministry Mean to Us Today?

". . . recovering of sight to the blind, . . ."

- How are we responsible for the physically blind?
- Besides physical blindness, what are some other ways people are "blind" today? (For example, people of one color willingly keep people of another color from enjoying *all* of life, or those well off keep the poor from having what they need to live.)
- How can we help correct these kinds of blindness?

The Proclamation of Jesus

". . . to set at liberty those who are oppressed . . ."

then

now

What Does Jesus' Ministry Mean to Us Today?

". . . To set at liberty those who are oppressed . . ."

- What does freedom mean to persons in our society?
- What do racism and the differences between poor and rich have to do with the oppressed?
- How are we as Christians responsible for the oppressed today?

The Proclamation of Jesus

"... to proclaim the acceptable year of the Lord."

then

now

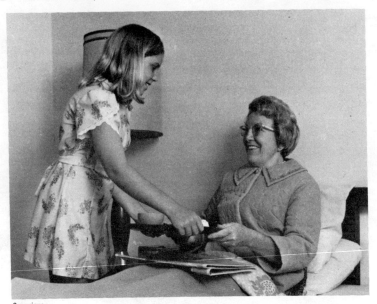

Camerique

What Does Jesus' Ministry Mean to Us Today?

". . . to proclaim the acceptable year of the lord."

- How can this proclamation happen in our day? (The "acceptable year of the Lord" means that God's rule brings justice and peace.)
- How can the people of God bring about the necessary changes to proclaim peace and justice today?
- How did Letha Wakeman and Leon Sullivan proclaim the acceptable year of the Lord?

Checklist: The Neighbor's Good

Here are some problems we face today. Mark the column which expresses your feeling.

A. I cannot do a thing.
B. I can learn more about the problem.
C. I can get others interested.
D. I can do something about it.

A B C D

1. When children in my school do not have warm clothing to wear—
2. When fathers are out of work because they lack the skill needed for the jobs that are open to them—
3. When I see minority groups moving into my neighborhood, and my parents and friends do not want to accept them—
4. When older people in my community are lonely, sick, or unable to get out of their homes by themselves—
5. When younger children or young people my age have a difficult time learning in school—
6. When my nation fails to conserve its natural resources—
7. When people in my community organize to work to improve the schools—
8. When the people in my church or community are not interested in giving money to help people in other countries—

Compare your answers with those of others, perhaps your pastor, parents, or friends. Talk over the questions. Think about: What do these questions mean in the light of Christian discipleship?

Some Things for You to Do:

1. Make a "People Portrait" of the members of your congregation who actively minister to the needs of others outside the church. Here's how:

   - Begin with a long sheet of paper, perhaps two yards long and one yard wide.
   - Look for items which describe the activity of individual church members, such as church newsletters, church bulletins, and newspaper articles.
   - Use words and captions either printed, written, or cut from newspapers to describe the activities, interests, and daily occupations of persons.
   - Use pictures of church members from picture directories your church may have, or visit people and take snapshots of them at work.
   - Find out about the missionaries who have gone out from your congregation or missionaries your congregation has adopted.

2. Take an inventory of the needs in your own local community.

   - What opportunities are there for recreation for young people?
   - How are the poor helped? What organizations operate to meet their needs?
   - What organizations or people are responsible for counseling troubled children, young people, and adults?
   - What kind of program is there for shut-in adults, lonely senior citizens, or the handicapped?
   - Is there a program for single parents in your church or locality?
   - How are homeless children cared for?
   - Is there a program to help retarded people?
   - What world relief programs are sponsored by your church or other local community organizations?

3. Think over
   - How can you be responsible for helping others in need in your community? List your ideas.

   MY PERSONAL PLAN FOR MINISTRY

   - Write your plan here and then check it out with your pastor.

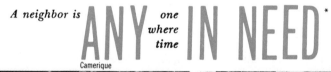

A neighbor is ANY one where time IN NEED *

Camerique

Bob Combs

*James Ashbrook, *be/come Community* (Valley Forge: Judson Press, 1971), p. 115.

7
Living As a Christian

In the other sections of this book, we have looked at the Bible, the church, heroes of the Christian faith, and the life of the Christian community today.

This section has to do with you. It helps you to examine some of the things that mean the most to you in life. It suggests ways you may set up a Christian life-style.

Some Things to Think About

What is most important to me?
What does living as a Christian disciple mean?
What will help me keep growing as a Christian?

What Is Most Important to You?

Imagine: An explosive fire rocks your house—you must leave right away, not a minute to spare—you have only time enough to take one person and one thing.

What one person in your family would you save?

What one thing in your household would you take with you?

These would be hard decisions to make. Think of what came into your mind as you wrestled, even in your imagination, with such a decision.

What would you say is most important for you?

What do you really prize above all else?

VALUES are what count most.

Values are used in our decision making.

> **val-ue: something desirable for its own sake; a value causes us to have a feeling or emotion.**

Looking at Your Own Values

The following paragraphs may help you think about some values. What do you feel most strongly about? Some people place a high value on owning certain goods. One person may "want" a motorbike and "feel good" owning and riding it. Another person may "feel good" owning tropical fish, or some books.

In the chart below, the statements are a way of helping you find out what means the most to you. Place a check mark on the line where it will describe how you feel. The value of how you feel is on a scale from 1 to 10; 1 indicates a low value or little interest, and 10 indicates a very high interest and a high value. You may check any number on the line that shows how you feel about each statement.

WHAT COUNTS THE MOST?

1   2   3   4   5   6   7   8   9   10
I like to be the best-dressed person in the group.

1   2   3   4   5   6   7   8   9   10
I want to be well liked by others.

1   2   3   4   5   6   7   8   9   10
I like people to think of me as truthful and honest, even though the truth may sometimes hurt others.

1   2   3   4   5   6   7   8   9   10
Buying and owning are important to me.

More Ways to Think About Your Own Values:
Write in your own words what you really feel about the following ideas:
What I look for mostly in my friends is

For me, to be successful means

By the time I am twenty-five, I expect to

Some of the people I admire most are

What I like about them is

I would consider myself a failure if

I would consider myself a success if

VALUES
Jesus Taught

An important value Jesus demonstrated was
CARING FOR OTHERS.
Jesus cared about persons. The Gospels tell us of the many different ways in which Jesus helped people who needed care.

What does caring mean?
To help a person who is hurt,
To comfort someone who is sad, or
To be company to a lonely person
are simple ways we can show that we care for another person.
List some of the people who have cared about you. How did they show their concern? Think of some people you value. What are some of the ways you care for them?

Jesus Was Sensitive to the Misfits of Society

Jesus was open to "oddballs." He cared for people who didn't fit just right into the social and religious patterns of his time. Here are a few you may identify through your Bible study:

Mark 2:13-17	Mark 7:24-30
Mark 3:1-6	Luke 13:10-17
Mark 5:1-13	Luke 19:1-10

The Values of Jesus Are Not Accepted by All People

There are people who say Jesus was a sissy and taught a softhearted way of life. Some people today insist that only might and strength can conquer. They argue that Christian concern for the helpless and the poor is a weakness.

There are many people today who do not even think about values. They live from day to day without choosing to be for or against Christian values.

Some get along on values inherited from their childhood. They do not consider what is right and wrong. Instead of choosing between good and evil, they may ask, "Can I get away with it?" Such a way of doing things is amoral. Amoral means to be without values by which one decides how to live.

Myself ⟵⟶ and Others

Jesus lived and taught certain values. To be a Christian means to live out these values. We learn what Jesus valued by reading the Bible. We also watch how others live who are trying to live by the values of Jesus. They may influence us.

Who are the persons who have influenced your life?

What are the specific ways they have influenced you?

The way persons relate to each other can shape and change them. You may remember one of your own experiences. Think of when you have seen this change happen.

Describe an experience when someone had gone out of the way to help you. How did it make you feel?

Describe when you had an opportunity to help someone. What did you do? How did you feel?

Think of someone you know. What can you say to that person that helps to make for good feelings? bad feelings? Here is a list of sayings. Which ones help a person? Which ones tear a person down?

Wow! That was okay!
You always goof!
You never catch on!
What can we expect from him?
Hey! That's okay!
How about helping me—you know how to do it.
Where did you get that outfit?
You are clumsy!

There are three MAJOR decisions every person makes sooner or later in life.

1. *Life Philosophy*

Think about:

What will I do with my life? By what standards will I judge the failures and successes of my life? What goals will I set for my life? Will I give my life to Christ? Will I judge my life by

> **phi-los-o-phy:** an overall attitude toward life; a guiding idea about the purpose of life for you.

goals such as fame, wealth, power? What *are* my goals?

You have begun to work out your philosophy of life now. You will continue to develop it throughout your life. As you grow, you will experience what it means to live as a follower of Christ.

2. *Life Partner*

The kinds of friends you have now may affect the kind of person you marry, if you decide to marry.

Think about:

What do I look for in my companions? What kind of home life do I want? With whom will I spend the bigger part of my life? Do I want to marry? Or will I remain single? What do I want in the kind of person I may marry someday?

3. *Life Work*

Choosing a career is an important consideration for both girls and boys.

What will I do in life? For what kind of career will I prepare? What kind of preparation will I need?

All three decisions—about your life philosophy, life partner, and life work—are related to your Christian discipleship. To be part of the people of God involves these major choices in life.

Planning Your Next Step

Discipleship is something unique. Each disciple discovers an individual style of discipleship. To follow Jesus is a continuing process of discovery. To be a disciple doesn't happen automatically. It is part of the lifetime process of becoming the best person you can be.

The word *disciple* means to follow the discipline of a master. Jesus Christ had some disciplines in his personal life.

Some disciplines you may want to work on:

Find a time each day to grow in your spiritual life. It helps for it to be the same time each day (early in the morning, during the lunch hour, on the way home from school, etc.). It may be spent

—in meditation,
—in conversation with God,
—in reading the Scripture.

Find a meaningful pattern, which may include

—reading Scripture,
—reading poetry,
—singing,
—a quiet time, or
—reading the prayers of others.

Develop study habits. Some suggestions are

—periods of Bible study on a regular basis,
—reading the life of Jesus,
—reading about the life of the church,
—reading about great religious leaders,
—writing your own poems, stories, diary, prayers.

Take a responsible part in mission.

—Be part of some caring group that undertakes to meet the needs of others. This may be a church group or organization in your neighborhood or town, such as the Scouts or 4-H.

—Be a regular part of some study group. This may be a church school class, youth fellowship, or perhaps both.

—Become part of the congregation. The living church carries out the healing love of Christ. It has need of workers. Find the place where you can be effective.

—A planned pattern of giving to the church is part of your discipleship. You may be limited in what money you have, but your gift each week or each month helps keep the church going. Your regular gift adds to the outreach of your congregation in missions.

Thinking Over This Study

The following statements may or may not be true. As you check the columns, think about what each question means. They will help you review this study.

	False	Partly True	True
1. Joining the Christian church means I become a part of the community of the people of God.			
2. Becoming a Baptist means I cannot be a part of any other denomination or faith.			
3. Baptists do not differ from other Protestant denominations in their beliefs.			
4. The Christian church is not responsible for what happens in the local community.			
5. Christians are responsible for what happens to other people in the world.			
6. Joining the church involves my taking part in the activities of the Christian community.			

Write in your own words:

⚫ The most important learnings I have discovered in this study:

2. The questions I still have about church membership and accepting Jesus Christ as Savior:

3. The next steps I will take
   • to continue learning:

   • to be involved in ministry: